S0-CRG-110

Resting on the Bridge

For Lorene,

who explored the still
places with me,

E M Cofer

Jeremiah 6:16a

RESTING
ON THE BRIDGE

poems by E. M. Cofer
illustrations by Margit Trautmann

Copyright © 2002 by E.M. Cofer
All rights reserved
Printed on acid-free paper

ISBN: 0-9649925-2-3 paper

Cover design and illustrations: Margit Trautmann

Cover photo: Charles Dare Hawley, the poet's father
Quote on page 48: taken from the diary of Elsie Barkman,
     the poet's mother
"Grammy's Kitchen": Previously printed in *Grammy's Kitchen*,
     by Jani Davis

Published by:
Hawley Court Press
P.O. Box 1191
Ottumwa, Iowa 52501

Printed in the United States of America

10 9 8 7 6 5 4 3 2 1

for the bridge builder

CONTENTS

INTRODUCTION

It wasn't until the house in which I grew up was leveled that I gave a great deal of thought to what happened there. By then the yellow rosebush, wafting its sweet scent through the kitchen window, and the bridge across the irrigation ditch, responsible for my concussion, were fading memories.

When physical landmarks are no longer visible, recollections of past experiences come to the forefront. This collection of poems touches upon foundations laid for me by immigrants, coal miners, preachers, teachers, carpenters, statesmen, and workers of the soil who taught me to find beauty in simple things, strength in a practical approach, and the sunlight of laughter even in difficult times.

A few remembrances have been inspired by others whose stories touched and changed me, for my connections encompass not only my extended family but dear friends and neighbors who have helped build bridges with me.

ARROWHEAD

Dad hands me the arrowhead he found
while plowing on the hill. I turn it over
in my hand, fingering flaked ridges
where someone chipped away at the stone.
I imagine tepees on the hill, a village:
mothers, fathers, dancers and drums,
children racing, chasing the wind.

Our farm shapes me.
Blizzards, droughts, hailstorms
chip away my rough edges.
The soil which absorbs
my footprints does not belong
to me. I belong to it. No matter
how far I roam, this beckoning land
continues to call me home.

WINTER STOREHOUSE

Down in Grandmother's cool cellar
on this side of the coal bin
rows and rows of canned tomatoes
and green beans line the shelves. Apples
rich with cider scent wait for pie crusts
and, at the foot of the stairs, oversized
crocks hold dill pickles spiced and salted,
sausage and headcheese. In the shed
with the cream separator, Grandfather
hangs sides of beef and venison.

On a chilly, fall Saturday
he hitches team to wagon
and drives seven miles to town
where he picks up twenty-five pounds
of flour, a sack of sugar, two boxes
of matches and some barbed wire.
Grandfather says they should
have a good winter if the hens
keep laying and the new cow
comes fresh in January.

GRANDMOTHER'S WORDS

I never sat at Grandmother's knee.
I never heard her stories
of far-off lands, seafarers or trolls
—old myths to help me understand
her early life, what it was like
to cross an ocean on her own,
nor could I grasp cradle tunes
crooned in another tongue.

It seemed she always hurried.
I watched the flurry of her hands
fashioning tatted lace
for collars on my dresses.

Ruffles, pleats and running lines
were Grandmother's soliloquy,
her handiwork a tapestry
and applique, her scroll.

LEGACY

My grandparents' parlor
had rugged elk antlers on the wall
and in the corner a velvet-lined
        pump organ.

These early Wyoming homesteaders
eked out sustenance
hunting deer, antelope, elk—
wasting nothing. A wapiti
hat rack hung on the wall.

But I wondered by what means
the pump organ came to this
        lonely spot.

When I was grown I traveled to Gotëland
meeting across-the-sea family,
with them strolled the churchyard
noting familiar names on slate
        gray stones.

Cont.

Together we entered the church,
a white sentry with the town growing
around it. There I saw
treasures in a secluded room
and a chiseled altar
          three centuries old.

An altar, intricately carved,
shaped by an artisan who carried
within his veins strains of the same
          genetic code as mine.

I beheld mastery
that echoed in Grandfather's
polished oak cabinets
and in flame-etched wood prints
          in the parlor.

Then I understood the need
for melodia, flute and reed
and comprehended art and faith
strong enough to tame
          a wilderness.

CHOKECHERRY HARVEST

Grandma is used to seeing us
in our Sunday best, but today
she's not surprised when ragamuffins
show up at her door. She hands us
pails for cherry picking.

Twelve cousins race together
to the thicket along the apple orchard
edge, throwing out a challenge
of who first can fill the bucket.

The dusty air hangs with fruity tang
so sweet we have to taste. Chokecherries
pop in, faces skew, tongues are numbed.

We compete with birds and swarming gnats
for fruit on cluster-laden branches.
We laugh a lot when Billy trips
and spills his near-full piggin.

We tell ourselves Grandmother needs
our toil and perspiration, but most of all
we harvest fun in summer celebration.

DUST ON THE LARAMIE PLAINS

Sometimes
the wind
blows so hard across
these upland plains
that I cannot see
my way.
A whirling
dust devil skitters
along the ground,
peppering the backs
of my legs with sticks
and anthill sand.

My nostrils, my teeth,
my hair, the folds
of my neck fill
with grit, and I wonder
who it is I carry
around with me:
residue of a long-ago
leather-clad warrior
a French beaver trapper
a cattle-drive cowpuncher
or antediluvian dinosaur dust.

CRYSTAL PARFAIT

Mama had parfait glasses
of fine, etched crystal
packed in a trunk.
I didn't know she had them
till my fifth Fourth of July
when she placed one before me
filled with layered cream
and strawberries.

We used them at Uncle Carl's
farewell party before he went to war.
On Anna's birthday one broke,
the first to return to sand.

Once Mama came to call
at my outdoor playhouse
bringing crystal glasses on a tray.
She sat erect in a rocking chair that
didn't rock, admired my child-made table
and its bouquet of wild sweet peas
in a jelly glass.

Cont.

I have lived other places, have
entertained other guests, but none
more honored than my mother
who entered my house of swept dirt floors,
leafy bough doorways and lofty blue ceiling
and sipped with me sweet-sour lemonade
from dewy parfait crystal.

LESSONS OF THE FIELDS

Mama says seven years old
is too young to work in fields.
Daddy says, "Don't you know
there's a war on?"

Today, he'll teach me
the difference between a weed
    and a bean.

The summer of '43
in a twenty-acre field
I learn about
    work and play
        oppression and freedom
           hatred and love
as Dad and I walk long rows
side by side.

IN THE DARK

We are all
   in the kitchen
      in the dark

breathing together
   leftover peppery smells of
      supper's fried potatoes

We can't see the light
   in the next neighbor's yard
      nor the house on the hill

We huddle as close
   as our Sunday morning snuggle
      in Mama and Daddy's bed

Cont.

Daddy sings softly
    "God Bless America"
        I hum along

He reaches for my hand
    covers it with his
        squeezes till it hurts

As we outwait
    a wartime
        blackout drill

PLAYGROUND

The ditch rider turned water off
a month ago—
        summer's end

Irrigation canal bed is
almost dry—silt sifting through
        bare toes

that run the track
with tumbleweed stallions
        racing the wind

THE CHRISTMAS DOLL

It wasn't much of a toy—
a porcelain doll so small
it fit inside a matchbox

One careless act
and it would break

Disappointment in my eyes
mirrored in my mother's

for that was all she had
to offer me

It was the year it hailed
and crops failed

and another baby
came to stay

and Edward R. Murrow
talked on the radio

Cont.

and everybody planted
Victory gardens

and did without sugar
cookies

That year I received a doll
with clothes so small
they were held together

by fragile, hand-sewn threads
of a mother's love.

TEMPUS FUGIT

On Easter Sunday
Dad sets the clock ahead
ten minutes. He knows
Mama underestimates
by just a little bit
how long it will take
to start the roast, to wash
a child's face, to get
the right flip on her hair.

Dad doesn't like to be late
for church, especially
on Resurrection Day.

TO DUST OR NOT TO DUST

Deer flies, houseflies, horseflies, beetles,
Irrigated fields with mosquitoes,
Grasshoppers, dragonflies, wasps and weevils,
Spotted, yellow bugs on potatoes,

Corn borer Lilliputians sawing stalks and shoots
With the vengeance of a ring-tailed bugaboo,
Grasshoppers spitting, cutworms at the roots.
Is there not a thing we can do?

We could ask that Stearman duster to exterminate
And get the buggy problem under control,
But there's more than cost we must evaluate.
Mama wonders about the oriole

Who just this year chose to hang its nest
In the front yard cottonwood.
She recalls early days living in the West
with no trees or bird songs. Then it's understood

That though she puffs a little dust on vines of tomatoes
And hangs sticky fly strips in the kitchen,
We will have to tolerate the gnats and mosquitoes
And just learn to live with the itchin'.

DAD'S QUIET TIME

Dad settles in his leather
high-backed rocker, unfolds
The Torrington Telegram
for his nightly read.
In overalls, end-of-day weary
he hides behind the newspaper,
the only time of day
he separates himself
     from us.

Our checker game is not going well.
My brother says I cheat and swats
checkers to the floor.
I throw a yellow No. 2 pencil
at him and miss. It arrows
through Dad's paper,
tears the article
     he reads.

He sharply rebukes us,
warns us of the danger of
irresponsibility. Dad disappears
again behind the paper, mutters,
"Can't a fella have a moment
     to himself?"

Cont.

He tries to read, through
ragged páper edges, an article
about the discovery
of a polio vaccine that might
    save his children.

CORNER GROCERY

We set up shop behind the garage
with shelves of bricks and boards.
Old apple crates with a plank across
formed the counter for our store.

We lined the shelves with empty cans
of tomato soup, looking new.
Mama's can opener had removed bottoms
so holes were hidden from view.

We sold empty cartons of eggs
and carrots from the garden,
nearly used-up pencils, dim batteries
and a pail we once used to put lard in.

We hadn't many customers
and most of them were us.
We paid with stones, broken rings
and washers brown with rust.

It rained one day on our outdoor store,
blew cans and crates about
and sogged empty cardboard boxes.
Most things we had to toss out.

Cont.

But that day, I made my biggest sale.
I shaped brown paper into a cone
and filled it with chocolate mud.
Dad said, "I'll have to have one."

He dug deep into his overall pocket.
It took him an awfully long time.
He paid me in full for that ice cream cone
with a shiny, new, Roosevelt dime.

WASHDAY

Monday mornings, I wakened early
to help my mother push
the galvanized Maytag washer
from the corner of my bedroom
to its place near the kitchen sink.
I filled the rinse tubs with cold water
from the faucet; Mama lifted steamy
tea towels from the copper boiler.
Together we poured hot water
into the washer, added whites
and waited while the agitator
chunk-a-chunked dirt away.
We lifted each shirt and sock,
puffed with water, and fed it
to the wringer, watchful of fingers.

The year I was tall enough to reach
the taut line, my mother and I hung laundry
with a basket between us. Singing
our "Clementine" duet, she hung towels
and I clothespinned washcloths
one by one.

Cont.

On March days, wind blew so hard
shirt sleeves wrapped round and round
the lines, refusing to let go.

In winter, towels and sheets freeze-dried.
Clothespins gripped icy corners
that had to be pried loose by fingers
stiffened with cold.

Half-frozen laundry finished
drying on racks and makeshift
lines strung from curtain rod to curtain rod
in the living room. Mama warned
the little ones to keep soiled hands
away from the whiteness.

This last load would not finish drying
till long after supper. All evening
rising steam transformed the room
into a magical maze, an off-limits
playground with a fresh sagebrush scent.

WINTER KILL

Today is an indoor play day
like the day Uncle Carl
robbed the beehive.
That day we four stayed
inside so we wouldn't be stung.
We sucked sweet
honeycomb all winter.

Today the uncles are here again
to butcher a hog. Mama says
children don't need to see such things.
We play, but our games turn silent.
We hold our breaths, listening
on this day of the year
Daddy hates most.
Tomorrow we'll visit the pigpen
to see which one is gone.

WHEN MAMA LEARNED TO DRIVE

We didn't know when Mama drove
into the grindstone, denting
the front bumper and setting
the grind wheel slowly turning,
that her foot refused to move.
Dad shook his head and said,
"woman driver." We figured she'd never
master the horseless carriage.

We didn't know that five years
down the road, Mama's leg would drag
when she walked. Doctor thought maybe
a stroke. Mama said nerve damage,
dating back to a runaway horse
before she was our mother.

We didn't know that twenty years later
and for the rest of her life, Mama
would drive a wheelchair.

HEADLINE: ARTIST LOST IN STORM

There was only one building
on the tired, old farm
that was worth saving,
but that was before the tornado
took it up in its arms
and smashed Norman Rockwell
against the trees.

We'd carefully swept
the concrete floors
after the grain was sold.
Each of us set up a household
in the granary which had held
wheat, barley and oats.
We could stay in these homes
safe from hail and rain
for one whole month
till combine and auger
refilled the bins.

It took two of us
to move the table
from our former home in the wood.

Cont.

No one complained: We were moving
to a ritzy neighborhood.
We had fixtures and pans and cans
and partitions on which to hang pictures.

Movie stars stared
from the wall on the south;
on the east were cowboys and fish.
But my apartment, far to the west
had only *The Saturday Evening Post's* best.

Then a storm threatened;
a cylone whirled.
We hid in the cellar
away from the wrath
Nature was dishing out
on the world.

And when we emerged,
that world was different.
Though our farmhouse still stood,
one thing was evident:
The Norman Rockwell I cherished
had perished.

SUMMERTIME

In summer, the center of our house moves
to the front porch which is really the back porch
'cause the back door has always been the front
        for most of our visitors.

When people come by now they never knock
'cause they can see by looking through the screen
        whether we're home or not.

There's a hook in the middle of the ceiling
but it's not used for anything 'cause the baby
grew up, and the swing doesn't hang
        there any more.

On the north end of the long porch is a cot
with a mattress which is usually folded back
so it won't get rained on which almost never happens
        in Goshen County, Wyoming.

From that cot, you can see right away
when the mailman comes,
but you don't bother to put down your book
and run along the path to get the mail
unless you see him lean out his car window
and stuff a Sears Roebuck package
        into the box.

Cont.

The bushel basket that peaches came in
two weeks ago is lined with newspapers
and has a chick in it, one whose mother
left him before he'd finished hatching.
We found him still in the nest,
wet and struggling, and now it's up to us
            to save him.

The best time of day is supper time
when the table we moved from the kitchen
to the porch is loaded with fried chicken
and ten kinds of vegetables from the garden,
and though you have to clean up your plate
you can choose what you put on it
            in the first place.

And summertime grace is a lot better
than wintertime grace 'cause birds
in the fields and trees
            sing along.

WATER FIGHT

It started with squirt guns—
three kids in a tub squirting
water up the green-tiled wall
of a turn-around small bathroom.

And Mom didn't care.
She said, "All's fair
in love and war."
Dad joined in

throwing on the wall
water from a paper cup,
and on the plastic curtain
were bubblesuds all the way up.

And Mom didn't care
about the mess in the tub
because a bathroom needs
a good, frequent scrub.

So in the mind of the smallest son
grew the concept that cleanness is
        necessary and fun.
Even a pet turtle shouldn't stink
and could use a sudsy bath in the sink.

Cont.

In this clean, tiled, sanitary room
the reptilian pet met his doom.
Though the battle with germs was won,
can cleanliness be overdone?

CHRISTMAS REFLECTION

The Denver Post article riled Dad.
It's content made him mad
enough to send the first communication
he'd ever written to a publication.

The article had complained about kids'
Christmas homecoming, bringing their kids
and racket, disrupting normal lives,
treading on grandparents' rights.

Dad couldn't comprehend the ingratitude
of one who wished to be alone
to wallow in his solitude
rather than welcome children home.

"I dread the day," his letter said,
"when mine are far from home,
or illness, death or circumstance
doesn't allow them to come."

He signed and sealed the letter
and walked the well-worn path
to the mailbox along the gravel road
and raised the signal flag.

Cont

The holiday came, and Dad gathered us in.
Mama burdened the table with food.
At dinner, we grasped each others' hands
and bowed in gratitude.

And after the feast, the wee ones
climbed upon their grandpa's lap
"Don't bother him," we parents said.
"Let Grandpa take a little nap."

"No, let them be," Dad said.
"Few of my days are so richly blest."
Then he proudly pulled out the Sunday edition
and showed us the page with his declaration

printed in *The Denver Post.*
I think that's when I loved him most.

GRAMMY'S KITCHEN

The back door is the way to Grammy's kitchen,
to chokecherry jell on corn bread, and lemon pie,
and laughter served with biscuits and vegetable stew.
New brides, new babes are greeted with spicy scents
of Christmas cookies, hot chocolate or pumpkin pie—
Welcome in the warmth of Grammy's kitchen.

Zucchini is growing quickly in the garden;
Grampa found another two feet long.
Harvest preparations in Grammy's kitchen
draw each new soul into the family circle,
canning quarts and quarts for winter's storehouse—
Initiation rites in Grammy's kitchen.

Little helpers stand on pulled-up perches,
kneading bread on flour-dusted table.
Love surrounds the dimpled-elbowed darlings
filling jar-lid pans with well-worn dough balls:
whole wheat bread to spread with apple butter—
Making memories in Grammy's kitchen.

Lessons are subtly learned in Grammy's kitchen:
Life is tough, but God's love even tougher.
The load is lighter, together, around the table
and sorrows can be eased by comfort food.
Hail that slashed the garden is making ice cream—
And rainbows can be seen in Grammy's kitchen.

CHERRY CREEK BRIDGE

Monday the bridge collapsed.
Samuel saw it on Friday and cried,
cried for its loss, raged at the swollen
stream that created the log jam, damming
up water like tears splashing his suit.

He had not wept while holding
his father's age-softened hand
hospital-sheeted as he slept,
nor for the satin-pillowed form
laid rest. But for the bridge

where first the father taught the son
to bait and cast bread upon water.
And under the bridge where he and Joe
found crawdads, shouted secrets
while strained, complaining planks above

shuddered under ladened sugar beet trucks.
The dancing bridge with headlighted cars
at each end, rock and roll blasting on the radios,
and Becky in his arms under the bridge,
dust drifting down on her freckled nose.

Cont.

The bridge had decayed while he was gone,
gone east to soar above the world.
The father had nourished the boy, praised him.
Samuel wept. Just one more time, he wished
he could have rested on the bridge.

MY CHILD

She left today.
White parka hood shielding her
against the cold, white fuzzy
dog tucked under her arm.
I watched her go.

My job is finished.
Other hands will shape her,
other minds judge her,
trim away the dross and make her
what she needs to be.

She left today
to meet another world
where others will read what they
think she is. She'll become
a thousand things
to fill their needs.

Is she strong
enough to survive their
definitions? Have I shaped
her well enough so she
holds fast, this little piece of me
thrown to the world?

SILENT RAIN

The door slammed shut.
You were gone.
Two travelers dead ended
at the crossroads.

In tomb-like silence
of an empty house, I sat
while torrents of rain pelted
down, transporting diluvian debris,
bringing renewal.

Like a lone parachutist
I drifted toward the rainbow,
holding fast to its promise.

SNOW THUNDER

"Joint custody," the judge declared,
and everyone said it was best
                 for the child
who knew he'd have mother
and father part-time.
In between they'd all pretend
the sun was shining.

He remembered when the storm began:
first a cloud, then spattering rain,
thunder and lightning.
And from the darkened sky
snow began to fall,
softly, slowly, flake by flake
piling up against the back yard

fence where he volleyed his tennis ball.
He could still do that. "Nothing's
changed," they said. "Love's the same."
He could bounce his ball at this home
or that, unless he forgot and left it
at the other place.

DRINK TO ME ONLY

Until you've tasted wine
in the wine district of Portugal
Until you've sat on a stool
in a cool cellar surrounded
by fruity kegs

Until you've sipped amber fluid
at a white-linened table
on a Parisian sidewalk
held hands and watched passers-by
created your own sparkling
island on the Seine

Until you've discovered
the friendliness of wine
in a California vineyard
sniffed the bouquet
sipped ruby port from a stemmed glass
you cannot know what Bacchus knew

For it is the one you are with
and where you are
It is drinking with eyes
as well as lips   It is sweet
conversation and still pauses
that mellow wine
in a very good year

GROUNDWORK

Brother and sisters return to the garden
through a lopsided gate, hanging
from one rusted hinge. They share
memories of their mother's tabernacle.
Each dewy, summer morning she had
partnered here with the Creator.

She always overplanted. Cucumbers,
melons and pumpkins sprawled over
the north half of the garden. The best years
she won blue ribbons at the county fair.

She never picked the strawberry patch clean.
She knew her children's habits, how their last stop
after a day's field work was the garden.
Each morning, she could see where they
uprooted carrots or plucked a ripening tomato.

Cont.

The brother remembers the garden's surprises,
the year his mother dropped eggplant seeds
into the soil. He was awed by the swelling,
purple fruit, though he claims no one liked it much.
The next summer in that spot bachelor buttons,
daisies and cosmos nodded blue and white and purple
greetings to those who came through the gate.

Their mother had insisted trees be planted
along the west side of the garden to shelter
corn and yellow wax beans from the merciless,
afternoon sun. The youngest remembers
what the oldest never knew, how some afternoons
her mother eased herself down to rest on the weathered
chair, leaning now on its broken leg against the elm.

"I wish we could turn back time," the youngest says.
The brother nods, "Set up the chair, mend the gate,"
but already his eyes see beyond it.

Cont.

Sisters and brother wend their way through
cockleburs and overgrown pigweed to the middle
of the garden where a cherry tree stands.
They tell each other how their mother labored
over this tree, how she fertilized and watered
year after year. But the roots seemed not deep
enough, a late spring frost nipped blossoms,
hail beat off green fruit, robins and orioles
stole the scarce crop before harvest. In time
the mother let it be as it wished.

This year in the garden, a fruitful tree
embraces summer's hungry birds and all
who seek solace beneath its shady branches.

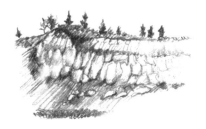

CANTABILE
for Don

This was the year
the maple leaves clung
to the tree all winter.
An early fall
shocked tender leaves
while still green. They
refused to let go
of what they knew
though the tree no longer
nourished them.

A sudden ice storm
enclosed each fragile leaf
in a crystal shaft.
Blustery gusts rustled
them like wind chimes.

Another spring will come,
another storm, another rainbow.
But I will remember
this year's buffeted chimes
and their soft, lingering echo.

SNOW PEACE

Snow is hushed, muffled, still.

Spring winds howl; summer rains drop
in drum-like rat-a-tats.
Thunder claps!
Hail beats a stony staccato
but winter's snow
    falls
        silent as sunset.

Only the young come out to play.

A sled glides softly
    down
        last summer's motorcycle hill.

White balls sail through the air
without the crack of bat.

The mail carrier and the neighbor's black dog
leave silent footprints
     in
       the
          snow.

NURSING HOME VISIT

Aunt Elvira, when you say
it is good of me to come,
I don't know how to tell you
why I need to be here.

I think back to the first time
I knew you. I watched you
slap bread onto the kneading
board and make a game of it,
your laughing blue eyes
meeting mine over the table.

I remember at age five when
I visited your home in the city,
how speeding cars scared me,
and you held my hand all the way
across the street.

Cont.

I remember that only you
could play the piano
without printed music,
and for all my years of trying
I never could quite
accomplish that feat.

When you talk, I hear
my mother's voice;
when you laugh, her laugh.
I wonder what it was like
when you were a child
sharing the part of her life
that I never knew.

Resolved: never to be afraid that I shall go too far in serving others, as there is no likelihood that any of us will be too bountiful, too kind, or too helpful to his neighbors.

... Elsie Barkman
(January 1, 1927)

New Year's Resolution: Entry found in the diary of Elsie Nelly Katrina Barkman who would, at a later date, become the poet's mother.

SOLITUDE AT SILVER LAKE

Silver Lake is lonely now.
Yesterday you stood here
dangling a fishhook in water,
lifting your eyes to azure skies
and snowy mountain tops.

Yesterday you skipped stones
on ripples, taking time to choose
the best, spreading circles
one upon another all the way
to the rock-lined shore.

I feel empty in this vastness.
When yesterday we shared it
I had found something big
enough, at last, to hold our love.
Today, I am too small to be noticed.

Cont.

I search for life among wildflowers
you taught me to identify, watch a bee
deeply drinking nectar of columbine.
I hear a rockchuck calling her babies
to safety. Too soon they will leave her.

Life in the mountains happens quickly.
In a few weeks the bee will be gone,
birds will fly south, snows will come.
Here at this mountain lake I pause
at summer's end, remembering you.

LIVING FOREVER

Sometimes we hear a song
read a poem
think a thought
that reminds us of one
who is gone

A tear comes
We are embarrassed
knowing others caught us
with our guard down
and can see how
vulnerable we are

Yet tears are a tribute
reminding us again
love remains
spanning distance
bridging generations

It gives hope
that we can live
forever
if we take time to touch
the lives of others

ABOUT THE POET

A native of Wyoming, Elsie Mae Cofer now resides in Ottumwa, Iowa, with her husband Larry. She previously taught in the Ottumwa school system and is the author of *Carrier on the Prairie*, the history of a World War II naval air station in Ottumwa.

As a teacher, mother, and grandmother, Cofer recognizes that each generation influences the next. Her predecessors include colonial patriots who established a new country and Swedish immigrant homesteaders who tamed the West. Their self-sufficiency, vision, humor, tolerance, and love continue to be sturdy planks undergirding the footsteps of those who follow.

ABOUT THE ILLUSTRATOR

Margit Trautmann was born in Kaiserslautern, Germany. Since 1995, she has made her home in Ottumwa, Iowa, working as a graphic designer and illustrator. Currently, she is employed by Chappell Studios of Fairfield, Iowa, which specializes in event photography. With her children Lisa and Tim, she enjoys swimming, boating, and camping with friends.

Trautmann's fondness for the West is captured in her illustrations in this book of poems. Riding horseback with her family through western canyons, locating Indian petroglyphs, and visiting caves with smoke traces left by Indian fire pits are among her most pleasant memories.